Broadax

AMY LAWLESS

BROADAX

AMY LAWLESS

OCTOPUS BOOKS

PORTLAND

DENVER

SEATTLE

FOR MY FAMILY

BROADAX

BY AMY LAWLESS

PUBLISHED BY OCTOPUS BOOKS

OCTOPUSBOOKS.NET

DISTRIBUTED BY SMALL PRESS DISTRIBUTION

SPDBOOKS.ORG

ISBN 978-0-9861811-5-3

FIRST PRINTING

DESIGNED BY DREW SCOTT SWENHAUGEN

ANNIE DILLARD

You must go at your life with a broadax.

UNWRAP A TIDY WORLD TO REVEAL A MESSIER ONE

Back in kindergarten once while snooping through my sister's desk drawer items, I found a balled up sheet of paper, which had been taped up into a ball with clear desk tape. Pressed into the furthest corner of the back of her desk. I knew it was a secret. Other items sifted through were baseball cards and doodles displaying her artistic talents. I looked at the clock. She wouldn't be back from first grade for at least an hour. Carefully, I unwrapped, so I could later fit it back into the same reckless, irregular ball. I flattened the sheet.

The paper read:

FUCK FUCK FUCK FUCK FUCK FUCK FUCK FUCK FUCK FUCK FUCK FUCK
FUCK FUCK FUCK FUCK FUCK FUCK FUCK FUCK FUCK FUCK FUCK
FUCK FUCK FUCK FUCK FUCK FUCK fuck FUCK FUCK FUCK FUCK FUCK
FUCK FUCK FUCK FUCK FUCK FUCK FUCK FUCK FUCK FUCK FUCK
FUCK FUCK FUCK FUCK FUCK FUCK FUCK FUCK FUCK FUCK FUCK
FUCK FUCK FUCK FUCK FUCK FUCK FUCK FUCK FUCK FUCK FUCK
FUCK FUCK FUCK fuck FUCK FUCK FUCK FUCK FUCK FUCK FUCK fuck
fuck fuck fuck fuck fuck fuck fuck fuck fuck fuck fuck fuck fuck fuck fuck fuck
fuck fuck FUCK FUCK FUCK FUCK fuck FUCK FUCK FUCK FUCK FUCK
FUCK FUCK FUCK FUCK FUCK FUCK FUCK *FUCK FUCK FUCK FUCK*
FUCK FUCK FUCK FUCK FUCK FUCK FUCK FUCK FUCK FUCK FUCK
FUCK SHIT SHIT SHIT SHIT SHIT SHIT SHIT SHIT SHIT SHIT SHIT SHIT
SHIT SHIT SHIT SHIT SHIT SHIT SHIT SHIT SHIT SHIT SHIT SHIT SHIT
SHIT *SHIT SHIT SHIT shit SHIT SHIT SHIT SHIT SHIT SHIT SHIT SHIT*
SHIT SHIT SHIT SHIT SHIT SHIT SHIT SHIT SHIT SHIT SHIT SHIT SHIT
SHIT SHIT SHIT SHIT SHIT SHIT SHIT SHIT SHIT SHIT SHIT SHIT SHIT
SHIT SHIT SHIT SHIT SHIT SHIT SHIT SHIT SHIT SHIT SHIT SHIT SHIT
SHIT SHIT SHIT SHIT SHIT SHIT SHIT SHIT SHIT SHIT SHIT SHIT SHIT
SHIT SHIT SHIT SHIT SHIT SHIT SHIT SHIT SHIT SHIT SHIT SHIT SHIT
SHIT SHIT SHIT SHIT SHIT shit SHIT SHIT SHIT SHIT SHIT SHIT SHIT
SHIT SHIT SHIT SHIT SHIT SHIT SHIT SHIT SHIT SHIT shit SHIT SHIT
SHIT SHIT SHIT SHIT SHIT SHIT SHIT SHIT SHIT SHIT SHIT SHIT SHIT
SHIT SHIT SHIT SHIT SHIT SHIT SHIT SHIT SHIT SHIT SHIT SHIT SHIT
SHIT SHIT SHIT SHIT SHIT SHIT SHIT SHIT SHIT SHIT SHIT SHIT SHIT

Each word in a different hand—yet still her own. Each pencil line by the same girl I had shared a bedroom with my whole life. She had never once uttered these words in my presence. We heard them when Mama burned her hand on the stove, or from Dada when the Red Sox dropped the ball (consistently). I shook. This was not what I expected. My hands unsteady, I wrapped it up again with fresher tape—not with the care for this world with which I had unwrapped it, but with a reckless horror of what the world was becoming

Broadax

I don't like it when men show anger. So I should tell you: the Incredible Hulk has terrified me for as long as I can remember. When I was a little girl, my parents watched the television show—and why shouldn't they?—it was about a nice guy who, when pushed too far emotionally, undergoes a transformation turning his molecules green and muscular and larger than life. With this new body and personality he solves problems absent of language, to varied results. When Bruce Banner "turned," I would scream at the top of my lungs and run (still screaming) and I'd sob clear across the house into something soft like a blanket or my trusted purple ragdoll bunny Bop for comfort. I'd cling and just let the sob exit my body so loud, like a spiritualist hacking out a representation of physical pain. Eventually, like everything in the Lawless household, this was turned into a joke. I aged a few years like everyone does over time, and my fear turned into a performance piece. I'd scream and run in jest at the mention of his name, and later my family obtained a Hulk Christmas ornament, which my dad hangs in the back of the tree every year so that I might not come upon it suddenly—lest I turn beast myself.

This Christmas my two year old nephew asked to be lifted to view the top of the tree. I lifted the kid and he studied the lights and touched each bulb with the robust persistence that earned him the nickname *Turdley* around the house. He touched his finger to the green monster and I mock dropped him and squealed *Hulk!* contorting my face into a rubbery grimace. He looked at me like *What the fuck?* and I said "Aunty Amy is afraid of the Hulk." But what does it mean to hold on to the fear of a mythical television character like the Incredible Hulk or even to the memory of this fear? The word "incredible" implies his very unbelievable and beyond-reason existence. "Hulk" is a word that means giant. He is an unbelievable giant. When something is not real, why do we fear it? The mind is a vessel shaped like a question mark. It waits to hold the impossible. I wait to hold the impossible.

The Incredible Hulk evokes sexism. He is a man with strength of both body and mind. In order to use the strength of one, he must turn off the other. Spigot. The voice is the mind exiting the body and when Banner is strong of body he can not speak. While Banner excels as a scientist, he's a bit of a pushover in his personal life. Blocked up, stuck, flaccid. I want to throw up because I don't know what to do with this information. When Banner returns to his original state, he is sometimes sick and weak from the after effects of radiation. He's hugged some toilets. His father killed his mother. He knows the rise and fall of the Oedipal sun.

Me: running and screaming.

When I was a girl, I had a funny thing to tell my father about on a Sunday morning—it was some joke that I knew he would like. I tiptoed in as quietly as I could and sat on a cardboard box that took my weight and said something like *Good morning, Dada. Guess what?!* In response, he made his voice extremely low to say ***BETTER NOT BE SITTING ON THAT BOX!*** and I became so very upset so quickly (as I was indeed sitting on that box), and his voice seemed angry in a way that did not seem to correlate to my behavior. I mean it was unexpected—and as a result I burst into tears and ran away refusing to be consoled even by my father's normal volume voice, my father's voice when he said he wasn't mad at me—he was *just kidding*. I remember hiccoughing again and again and making everything wet with my eyes until someone said I was being silly. Boxes aren't intended for sitting upon. Dads prefer more sleep on weekend mornings. And little girls with jokes on their tongues are always so very awake.

I am listening to a tape of my four year old self retelling the story of *The Three Bears*, a story riddled with inaccuracies. Hearing my past small voice puts me in tears before I even hear my narration of the bears leaving the house. Halfway through telling the tale I started conflating chairs with beds and hot with warm with cold. I yelled *MAMA I MADE A MISTAKE*. Though you can't hear her voice on the recording, my mother told me to just keep going. I kept going. A rendering of the house would make it four stories high with four levels of sub-basements. Goldilocks would either find hot porridge or warm porridge, chairs or beds, soft or hard. Eventually the bears came upon the girl asleep in the baby bear's bed. I ended the story there. *Mama I'm all done*, my voice wavered. Listeners of the tape will never know how the bears and the girl resolved their conflict. Goldilocks is my favorite squatter in all of literature. *Mama I'm all done*. At age four, I could not read. This was the best I could do for my favorite squatter. I didn't know how to end the story. Generally in retellings, Goldilocks is confronted. Sometimes she falls upon her bottom as she runs from the bears' home. Always the bears stand in their home somewhat confounded by what just occurred. Over time, many retellings have scraped away any hint of very real menace that a household intruder actually signifies: she's blonde, young, and vulnerable.

Senior year of high school my friend Karin took me and our friend Jill to Tuscon, Arizona to visit her aunt and uncle during spring break to check stuff out and explore. We were band nerds so don't get excited. It was mostly hiking and music and a goth club. We came back just as Boston pale as we left. One day Karin's uncle, who was pretty cool, told us that a few years back he and his wife had gone on vacation and he happened to get back to the house a few hours before his wife on the day of their return. While they'd been gone, a neighborhood young man with a developmental disability had run away from home and been squatting all week at their house, eating their food and watching their cable TV and masturbating naked all week in his own shit. Shit was smeared all over the walls. He pointed to where I was sitting on the couch and said *He was sitting right there Amy, right there where you're sitting when I took a frying pan and knocked him unconscious. The only reason I was able to do so was that he was jacking off so intently and focused that he didn't hear me come in. Shit everywhere. We had to get the place redone.* New couch? I asked. *Nah, we just got a new slipcover.*

Goldilocks is known for being poor, beautiful, vulnerable, and charming. Even so, she needed things to be *just right*. The Tuscon squatter made things just right by smearing his own feces, and engaging in a constant, urgent sexual self-gratification. He was also perfectly able to use the can opener. I remember asking my friend's uncle what the young man was running away from. I remember feeling satisfied with the answer: he was just disturbed.

On that same couch I watched the news of the Oklahoma City Bombing, which occurred the week I was in Tuscon. Shit smeared everywhere. I think of shit smeared thick onto a dick like paint to a canvas. Timothy McVeigh was blonde and poor and vulnerable. He wrote: "Go ahead, take everything I own; take my dignity. Feel good as you grow fat and rich at my expense, sucking my tax dollars and property." As an outsider, we can't know for certain how he felt. Seems vulnerable to me. He also always had trouble impressing the ladies. It was, in his opinion, his biggest problem until he started thinking about Waco. It's also safe to say that he lacked the charm of Goldilocks.

Žižek writes it was hate—pure and simple. And how McVeigh and 'bad' men like him are ready to ignore their own well being if they can, through personal sacrifice, deprive others of their enjoyment or even their lives. *If I can't have you then no one will* is a clichéd trope in one hour television dramas, an idea held—even in insanity—by many villains who kidnap. Think of the woman tied to the train tracks by a moustache-twirling, sniveling villain or the femme fatale with *don't-make-me-do-this* tears in her eyes aiming her gun at her ex after being jilted. Some people find and use a store of resilience following a personal or social humiliation to aid survival. Some don't or can't. As I write this on a moving train toward Boston, the geographical setting of my own relationship horror show, it is the 19th anniversary of the Oklahoma City Bombing to the day, April 19th. More than ever I feel I am—to quote Philip K. Dick paraphrasing Yeats—"an immortal soul tied to the body of a dying animal."

I also think about what was on the television that got the Tuscon intruder off. It was definitely daytime television. Certainly the news couldn't have gotten him hard. I like to believe it was something that represents our consumer driven culture, a metaphor for how sick we are in our modern times like *The Price Is Right.* His eyes would have settled in the middle distance between his self and the screen, the wheel turning and turning and slowing to just... the... right......spoke.

I wonder if I could knock a person unconscious if he intruded upon my space. Would I "turn" in time? They say we are stronger than we give ourselves credit. We surprise ourselves. Once my friend Sara got drunk and moaned in the spare bed at our apartment. We decided she needed to make herself throw up in order for her to get some sleep. *Should we make her smell her own vomit?* I offered. This was not helpful. I worry that in an emergency I will be neither wrong nor helpful. In an emergency will I be able to gather myself into a storm of violence?

A copy of the hate book *The Turner Diaries* was found in McVeigh's car. I had the distinct displeasure of reading this book in an upper level journalism course in college, and I will say that McVeigh was not having any love if he was reading this book. Reading that book is a lonely affair, one in which erotic energies are sucked into a ceiling fan only to be hacked into corporal bits & pieces back onto the reader. Charles Babbage, father of the computer, wrote "if you put into the machine wrong figures, will the right answers come out?" He concluded, no, the right answers do not come out. *Garbage in, garbage out.* Love keeps us humane. Human connectedness keeps us sane.

I just re-watched news footage in the aftermath of the Oklahoma City bombing and was reminded how many children were killed that day. Does a ceiling fan swing above you tonight? Garbage in. Garbage out.

In the film *Willie Wonka and the Chocolate Factory*, protagonists Charlie Bucket and Grandpa Joe stole and drank Fizzy Lifting Drink and were lifted, at first flying free with abandon, and then quite terrified toward a giant ceiling fan & certain death. Charlie whined, *It's pulling me in. I can't stop. There's nothing to grab on to. We're going to get killed.* Thankfully, Grandpa Joe discovered that burping resulted in a lowering toward the ground. They burped and burped, joyful to remain living and returned to the floor. The burping sounds were farty and therefore comic. *From now on we keep our feet on the ground*, said Grandpa Joe. I was relieved to not see bits of Charlie everywhere strewn red for the petty theft. The correct thing occurred. A boy is taught a lesson: he returns the infinite, Everlasting Gobstopper. The right people shook hands, the Earth enjoyed another twirl on its axis, and somewhere, someone is enjoying a chocolate bar. Yet we aislewalk to wed annihilation. Sure, laugh – but even I wear white & walk slowly.

When Grandpa Joe said we should keep our feet on the ground, might he mean something of logic? Might he mean blah blah blah humanity blah blah? Do you think he's talking about earning what's yours or about retribution? Grandpa Joe, a fiscal conservative in the classic sense. *Post hoc ergo propter hoc, my boy?* Burp ergo fart ergo living. Do you think Grandpa Joe meant anything aside from the physical location of his feet in space at that moment in time? How must it have felt, emotionally, for the commuters at the New Brunswick, New Jersey station who were hit with bits of the person who jumped in front of the train that recent day? A high dry cleaning bill for being in the wrong place. A high dry cleaning bill for not stopping a willed human action. A high dry cleaning bill for nothing. Proximity was their only sin and for it they were forced to see red. Me? I'd trash all the clothes head to toe. That or I'd think "This is the suicide outfit" each time I wore even a part of that ensemble. Every time I wore that coat or socks or shirt or shoes or pants or hat or skirt or glasses or sweater or bra or undies or thong.

Teach me to burp. I can't find anything to grab on to. Hold me. I'm taking me too seriously.

On the B side of the tape Molly recorded a screed, public for my death, my end, urgently and quickly. Her voice was high-pitched, cartoon-like and thus impossible to take seriously... even now in this age of routine school shootings and random, meaningless violence. But yes, it called for "The End of Amy." But listen, I *was* kind of lame. I couldn't draw very well. My chubby thighs encouraged giggly pinches from grandparents and hairdressers. I couldn't ride my bicycle in a straight line. I had no unique talents aside from my charm, my chubs, and my near perfect vision. She was an artist, athletic, had a gap between her two front teeth and wore 1980's big brown round glasses to correct her crossed eye. As a toddler she was once mistaken for Elton John at a gas station. It never occurred to me that this was anything other than perfection and wonderful. I loved her and thought she was God. Her opinion was divine, the word.

Seniors get high. Freshmen don't. McConaughey is mostly silent. Can you be the girl with the swishy hair and the space between her teeth? In two separate cars, intimacy is nearly impossible. People need to come together in the night. Dorks everywhere. I'm just trying to be cool. Chicks don't want to hear *anything*. Matthew McConaughey puts his thumb to the bridge of his nose, bends his neck, and laughs like *you have no idea what you're talking about*. He then gives a brief lecture on patience. The lecture is pretty incredible. See, patience is the ability to be calm and not annoyed when waiting for a long time or when dealing with problems or difficult people. It's nearly impossible.

The yoga teacher invites me to perform three warrior postures during class. I could do them in my sleep. These poses represent the universal enemy, any enemy, known and unknown battles fought, any battles. I laughed on my way to class today thinking about my big ass and breasts at war, civil or martial. Cushions, but so I went! My ideal is the Warrior Three, peaceful warrior. I stretch my spine and open up.

Older siblings are often godlike to those of us newer to Earth. Though they have experience, they refrain from the oppressive rhetoric of parenting. Her suggestion strikes me now as pedagogical in nature. *Die now.*

So when she would call for my death, it hurt, but was not *really* seriously questioned. I quietly figured I'd have some time to appeal to the authorities. She was probably right. Her shit didn't stink. Her feet didn't touch the ground. Her body looked like a body was supposed to look while my body housed mortal flaws, but as her sister I had a gift of providence: her proximity.

In school kids were nice, but I didn't trust them. I saw that some peoples' siblings walked them home, gave them hugs—*sincerely liked them!* But none was a true artist like Molly. None was worthy of worship.

The first time my mother told me I was patient I nearly lost my mind because I thought she was telling me I was at that moment in the hospital as a *patient* even though I was in my bedroom. Then months later she and my dad gave my sister a keychain that read Patience in red and gold above the cutest, greenest turtle that you could possibly imagine. I was insanely, lustfully jealous of this keychain. My eyes watered and I asked my parents why I was not given the Patience key chain and said life was not fair and it took forever for them to explain that patience was not the particular virtue I had to work on. Maybe I had to work on the crying or the jealousy or on the phonics skills. They said Molly had to work on her patience. I thought that if I'm so good at patience, then I should be given the keychain as a *reward*. But that's not how the pedagogy of parenting works. Parents don't get it. I'm still waiting for my fucking keychain. But McConaughey's lecture? He just says patience twice. He says "Patience. Patience."

Once in second grade, we were handed a photocopied drawing to "color in" during an art class. It was a drawing of a dog dressed in human clothing that my sister had hand drawn the year before following a routine session of teachers' worship of Molly. When I recognized her hand, I put my crayon aside and said "I refuse. My sister drew this." My teacher and I made awkward eye contact for more than a few seconds. I wish I'd said it in French, but I was seven: *Je refuse! Je refuse! Je refuse!*

Around this time Molly spelled the word ‘chief’ wrong in the third grade spelling bee. This was her first known error.

I started to write *Molly* on window condensation whenever I found it alone & exposed. *Molly* in the kitchen, *Molly* in the car. I'd control my hand neatly, going against lefty instincts. This was my first lie. Nothing felt so honey as my mother's whine: "Why would Amy write *your* name?" Why indeed!

We creaked toward adolescence, and one day we sat doodling and reading at the kitchen table while our mom was out at the grocery store, surely cherishing her stolen moments away from us. Suddenly, I felt a sharp flick to my right temple, and immediately saw red, felt pain. I saw the rage of Achilles. I saw the blood rush forth from aging, gated waters. I saw the forked tongue of my sister pleased at inflicting pain in me, and I saw the shine of a very annoying apple. And I rushed toward her seeing it all. I hit her like the southpaw I'd loved and watched in the movies, got her in the gut. She didn't see it coming. She started walking backward and calling *Mama!* and *Stop stop stop!* and *What are you doing?* I continued hitting, punching, smacking.

Mama's not here, I answered. I hit her arms, smacked her shoulders, hitting widely at her, hitting "like a girl" but hard, with meaning. She walked backward, I hoped, with some regret. She held her arms crossed in front of her face. She looked pitiful. But she'd watched those boxing films alongside me. She knew how to protect her body. But she wasn't fighting back, and she was smaller now—Wizard of Oz after the curtain pulled open by Toto—this was no God, no Word. This was just a crying girl. But I could not stop, and I wasn't that much shorter than her anymore. I got a few more good ones in, and I was sobbing too. I was crying for both of us. I didn't want to hit her. I loved her more than anyone, and now I'd beaten her right up to the window three rooms past where we'd started in the kitchen. Then I saw through my red that one more hit would push her against the window and possibly harm her, so I did that thing I'd seen in the movies: I pushed my fist right up to her face and stopped a breath away from her eyes and said *Never do that again.*

The wonder of being able to, as a primate,
gather information.
Culling from ink on paper is a miracle
I guess.
It's a miracle I'm standing up. It's arguable.
Once I said "It's arguable"
and this dude was like
"You've been reading theory lately, haven't you?"

Walking toward a birthday party on an empty street
alone at night in Bushwick I thought
"I've never been so alone in my entire life."
Then a man asked me for a buck in earnest.
I ignored him.
He was the same person who, a few moments later,
pointed me to the unmarked and hard to see entrance to the bar.
Why did he acknowledge me when I did not acknowledge him?
And why didn't I open my wallet after he exhibited a soft human kindness?
To confirm the existence of another person—as a body in open space—
is a very basic validation. His body exists in space. There is money in my wallet.
FUCK FUCK FUCK FUCK FUCK SHIT SHIT SHIT SHIT SHIT SHIT

What is this violence?

I could offer some small and real defense about being a woman alone
on a dark street at night and the protective & invisible walls
I've built up around my body, but I choose not to.
How can I be more precise? It's not about description.

I want to be a better person.

So I knot it out   so that I might then negate.   I resist (it's kinda my thing)
May I argue that much of what I do is incorrect?

Then it fell from the sky!
Prince performed for eight minutes on television
backed by an all-female band. He made a statement about art
using art as his medium.
Women's bodies made sonic beauty.
His message was, as usual, about love   lovemaking   that slow release
eye contact
waiting, luxuriating   with a lover
He used a guitar to convince me   to find a new lover   (it's kinda his thing)
eight minutes, downhearted, but taking this time was in pursuit of beauty,
    the universal

There are so many beautiful ways to express the human body while it is still alive
Prince's guitar and his voice express this unprotected rage : the rage of
temporal enclosure

Maggie quoted from "Purple Rain" to me via text this week
during the endless conversation that is our friendship
She used the Prince lyric to explain
her perspective on an issue we were discussing
I listened to Purple Rain on repeat walking home from a spinning class
in Union Square to better understand her wisdom, which is vast
Around the fifth time, the words lost their meaning
and Prince's guitar was a dot matrix printer in my ear
and I was the vessel sound poured into
I stopped for a moment in front of the sushi place on 2nd Avenue
where a date brought me five years ago
Everything he said that night was delivered with a laugh
as he tried to classify each of my behaviors
Like having a work ethic was *such an Irish Catholic girl from Boston thing to do…*
and being so nice to my friends and drinking so much with poets …
I've forgotten what that was supposed to mean…something about the working class
He said it all with a laugh as a way of apologizing,
to soften being the dick that he was.
Then he ordered a quail egg on top of some sea urchin.
That was so funny to me and I didn't try to classify it. I just laughed.

Momma's boy with a trust fund who only works 10 hours a year
I mean, it was just another item on the menu.

Each morning I take a tincture of an herb into my mouth.
I baby bird my lips tight & chase it with water.
If I take the tincture I am able to laugh & be amenable
and so, the imperfections of the world are beautiful.
Without the herb I am unable to smile
unless things are really fucked up.
There's no right way to be.
For ten years after my grandmother died,
my grandfather sat in front of his TV not smiling—not even during Star Search.

What if I were to drag two bleeding suitcases
to the park after taking a cab there
pulled these two bleeding suitcases out of the trunk

How many times have I smiled, barking, lugging my suitcase through Penn Station:
"No I don't need help. I got it!"

Cab drivers are used to crazy shit   seeing shit from all angles
They cruise through
improbable memoir
I might even be dragging these suitcases as I wander the Earth's circumference

a planet across which I move ever-so-slightly for I am small

I can't see the curve of the Earth

I have no perspective sometimes

Well what's in the suitcases? you might ask.

It's not important. That is not the right question.

Or maybe it is—you ask good questions.

What is the difference between what an eye sees willingly

and what that same eye sees when the eyelid is being pulled, the skin,

the skin is being pulled by hands other than one's own   forced really

and directed to look at a *certain specific thing*.

And further, well, some people wear glasses, there is such thing as a lens

this lens is worn in front of the eye in order to adjust/change what the brain perceives

in front of the body in which it is held. I am one of these people, sobbing.

What good is curating my environment—what good is any of it—

if my environment must be curated.

I love it when my friends email me Youtube videos!!

My mother hears differences in my laughter.

When I laugh at something that that is 'knowing' or unkind,

the laugh has a certain sonic quality.

When I laugh at something that is humorous and kind or even sad
it sounds another.
Sometimes she calls out *Stop being mean* to my sisters and I from across the house
when all we're doing is laughing at animals on Youtube.
Like the video of the pig eating cookies after a nap—one of my favorites.
But my mother is never wrong in her classification.
Phoebe the pig, you see, sleeping in her own bed,
wakes up because her human had placed a cookie near her nose.
The smell aroused her and she ate with enthusiasm and pleasure
while the blanket continued to cover her big head.
She basked in her post-nap cookie.
The plot is unkind because Phoebe was taunted
out of her chubby innocent sleep to soothe the human's knowing wink.
The camera shakes due to Phoebe's human's laughter.
Watching a pig eat in bed under a soft duvet reminds us
of our own constant human gluttony.
And yet in some soft fleeting way we'd all like to be treated like Phoebe.

My head is thereby held half an inch from the ground,
the folded flesh above my eye is pulled taut—don't worry.
This does not cause me pain—it is just slightly uncomfortable.
This summer a spider bit my eyelid in a town called Shady, New York.
The skin around my eye swelled & was pulled taut.
I thought, well this is it: this *grotesquerie* is my new face.

"I live here now," I said to myself quoting a title of Jackie's
as I stared at this new alien. I pulled the hot flesh away
from my eyeball to try to find the person
I used to make eye contact with in the mirror.
She wasn't there anymore.
Eventually the swelling went down.
I am reminded once again that I am, as Yeats wrote:
"sick with desire / And fastened to a dying animal."

This is how I was then presented with the bleeding suitcases
of a cannibal from Japan, Issei Sagawa, who walks free,
his stuffed-animal fixation,
his conflation of sexual desire with his appetite for sustenance,
his head which was slightly too big for his limbs
as though two bodies were Frankenstein'ed into the body of one.
He could only speak of his carnal desires in his native tongue,
and the simple childlike joy he took from his material possessions,
his bewilderment, the wall-sized posters of Japanese women.
Like if you were to hang up blown up posters of your favorite foods
(hamburgers? chicken? soup?) floor to ceiling.

Your mouth is ball-gagged and you are tied to a bed. Your eyes are held open.
You love it.

O pretty please agree with me: there *are* limits to human empathy.
In watching I am forced to attempt to overlay my ideas about humanity
on top of his and I can not. He's a different kind of animal than I.

I am not so vast.

I am satisfied that I value human life.
This cannibal walks around day-to-day in a suit
hugging stuffed animals and marveling & laughing at his kitsch.
It's always a Saturday if you're a narcissist psychopath.

Endorphins are released in my brain in my prefrontal cortex.
This reaction occurring in my brain makes me laugh a little
in the privacy of my bedroom.
My brain tries to make sense of something that doesn't match up.
I mean, well, that's what Wikipedia says causes laughter.
But it's not funny.
Devaluation of human life and eating humans is not funny.
Once I wrote a poem about cannibals getting married.
People laugh every fucking time I read it.

A lover once announced to me that I laugh in my sleep.
I was not surprised.
I laugh, I giggle, and I cackle.
My brain tries to make sense of some things that do not match up.

While going through the ‘free box’ at work

I found Yukio Mishima’s novel *Confessions of a Mask.*

I emailed my friend a passage from the novel in connection

to a conversation we were having—he had recently introduced me

to this writer’s life and work.

He is drawn to controlling one’s human form and how Mishima

made his body into a perfect physical specimen

before committing ritual suicide… the human will as experiment. I quoted:

> *“…he represented my first revelation of a certain power, my first summons by a certain strange and secret voice. It is significant that this was first manifested in me in the form of a night-soil man: excrement is a symbol for the earth, and it was doubtlessly the malevolent love of the Earth Mother that was calling to me.”*

He wrote back *We should listen for and follow our Earth Mother.*

Did he mean that people should shit without prudence,

die, and then be buried thus return to the lover’s embrace

of the land on our only planet, Earth?

Isn’t that what humans are already doing: shitting and dying all over the place?

Making a blank of it all?

Some things hold more power than an individual can: the pull of nature, shitting, mothers, appetites, and time.

I like to think of defecation as a firm imperative, an exclamation point!

The digestive system starts at the mouth and ends at the ass.

Or does it start at the eyes and desire, extending through the hands?

Or does it start with vegetable farming and animal husbandry?

Hands are desire.

But I must insist that the digestive system ends at the asshole. End stop.

Game over.

What if the Earth really were your mother?

Is explosive shitting how your mother calls you?

Sometimes this call is inconvenient.

It comes at the wrong time.

Farting is the ring of an elegant doorbell.

A signal of what may be on its way to you.

"She's here!"

When I go to acupuncture, my pulse is felt.

He looks at my tongue.

My pulse is felt again.

He asks me about my bowel movements.

I say "actually I uh…a little diarrhea" and avoid eye contact.

I always explain the diarrhea or loose stools away to him with statements

like *I was nervous* or *I had some beer last night* or *I ate some street food.*
I will never surrender a narrative of my body's native messiness,
for that contrasts with the bright clean asshole of my hetero-normative
female affect.
I deserve more diarrhea for that last sentence.
My acupuncturist gives me corrections accordingly, tells me he has a girlfriend
and quickly feels my pulse once again.
And I am then sent into a nap with needles in my flesh.
I am given herbs.
I listen to a Pandora channel without commercial interruption
and am then charged a fee.
Each time I float onto the sidewalk afterwards wondering
whether my voice was accidentally lilting with the music of girlish flirtation.
My pulse is a three-lane highway.
Certain exits are blocked due to traffic.
Other exits are opened up, blood cells speed on the autobahn
of my veins and arteries.
I laugh a lot especially when I'm flirting
but this is due to the joy and humor expressed in human connection.
My blood has to go somewhere.
Here is finally some physical proof that I have a heart.

The call of nature is a euphemistic idiom meaning the need to urinate or defecate.
Everyone answers this call.

To not answer the call would speak to non-working human plumbing,
which would lead to disease and/or death.
When someone farted in my childhood home or in the car,
my mother always said "Who dropped a rose?"

Sometimes it was her! *She who smelt it dealt it.*

"Who dropped a rose?" is another euphemistic idiom that
– while familiar to me – always induces laughter in my friends.
I always imagine a beautiful woman
in a prairie gal high-collared, white lace dress
clutching two-dozen long stemmed
and thorny red roses running through the field.
Who am I kidding? I am this woman.
I rush through a field on my way to an important meeting and
I dropped a rose.
I no longer smell as good as I did a few minutes ago.
Instead of twenty-four roses I hold merely twenty-three.
The doorbell rings.
It is your mother.

Some people love to know who farted.
As if it would make a difference in how each smell were understood.
There is a correlation between the identity of the agent of the fart

and another person's willingness to stay in the room.
A mother catalogues information about her children
and their health and well-being.
But what of such fart cataloguing within other social groups?
Or is it a sport to know who is being called by
"the malevolent love of the Earth Mother" and how?
Everyone is called by such explosions.
However, some are more strategic as to where they let their flowers fall.

My mom calls and leaves voicemails.
How many times did she wipe my ass clean
and affix me with a new clean diaper
when I was a baby before I was toilet trained?
So many.
To envision a montage of this is both
overwhelming and tear inducing.
My mother's ceaseless attention to my body's cleanliness
in infancy and toddlerhood is something
I never considered when I was being a shithead
to her as a teen.
You don't get it! You don't understand me! (Door slam)
The song I would play watching a montage of my mom
cleaning me throughout infancy is "Beautiful Day" by U2.
I want to see her look at me clean again with eyes of wonder.
What's your montage's song? "Whoomp There It Is."

Shitting and energy acquisition are connected.
When I need additional energy to run my body, I must eat food.
My body metabolizes this and the excess is transformed into feces,
which must exit my body.
This is sometimes a convenient and zesty experience.
The process of writing about shit sounds tasteless,
but I am just answering a call, dude.
It's a beautiful day.

I watch a video of an xray of a female alligator breathing
& sit soothed by this cycle and set an intention
To watch the alligator video whenever I want to
To remind myself of who I am and what I can do
Without ever having to think about it
An alligator lung performs uni-directional air flow
Humans have bi-directional lungs
Which means that not all the air leaves our lungs each time we exhale
Something sticks around

I was a child hanging out on a tennis court somewhere in Boston.
My family members were playing tennis.
I was bored watching them play.
It was one of those devastating, doom-cloudless sunny days.
I was six or maybe I was seven years old.

I peeped a moving accumulation of a substance near mid-court near a
  chain-link fence.
I walked closer. A huge party of ants paraded toward a fallen lollipop.
I watched them march toward the candy.
Their marching seemed to have no mind.
I thought of how my mom would say *You can't just eat candy.*
I thought of my mom telling me to eat a piece of fruit.
Maybe the ants didn't know about healthy food choices
if they bombarded this lickable lollipop with such abandon.
I jumped upon them and stepped and killed some ants with my sneakers.
I jumped up and down. I didn't think they were anything.
I didn't think about them at all. I didn't think.
They stopped. They turned and gestured toward each other.
Silence. I saw some ant heads turn to the side
as if what they saw before them was some mistake.
They ceased this march toward the perfect, sun-baked lolly.
They began the collection of the bodies.
Some paraded away the bodies to protect them.
No one, nothing approached the lollipop.
I was a monster.
I watched them for a long time. I watched them carry.
I watched them return.
I saw the careful funerary procession.
Tim O'Brien wrote: *They carried the sky. The whole atmosphere, they carried it, the humidity, the monsoons, the stink of fungus and decay, all of it, they carried gravity.*

I watched the ones who left return.

I watched why an ant has to be able to carry 50 times its weight.

Soldier or ant, what's the fucking difference? I cried.

Amy what are you doing?

I hated myself for this monstrous act.

Humbled, I guess. Changed and I never killed again like this.

But what makes a human? What is special about this shape?

A child's sneaker blocks the sun on its descent.

The Earth Mother collects my excrements end to end.

Blood leaves my body
I'm both carrying and inside of a suitcase
SHIT SHIT SHIT SHIT SHIT
The blood gathers into a brand name
piece of cotton on a string connecting
me to both the Earth's umbilical
and a landfill's landscape

I stare at my right hand on which a scab heals
from some roughness I encountered while living

I spit some phlegm into a piece of soft tissue paper
for I am chronically ill and always dying a little

It's a miracle I don't yell at the dudes kicking my seat
on this commuter train
But more so, it's a miracle how
I'm out of bed making meaning on ink on paper
I enter the command   File → Print
And the printer still sounds like Prince's guitar

The Private Lives of Deer

When the wolf and the deer look at each another, they both like what they see. The deer is a mirror giving in to his reflection. He doesn't think of consequences. The wolf sees things as they are. When the wolf and the deer fall in love, it's real. The wolf anticipates her lover's every need. Some deer are selfish as fuck. But not this one. See: deer love a good narrative and love taking charge of building one. He loves wooing, preying upon the wolf, and also protecting her. The wolf changes shape into any chalice. You know, like a thesis statement. The deer is direct, a hook. The wolf understands and responds to this passion—probably on her back. Jupiter allows this trouble to unfold like a letter inside an envelope inside another envelope inside a bubble mailer. You've heard of "rock, paper, scissors"? Well, this is more like "paper, paper, paper" because both are writers and would resent all other conclusions.

I have your lending-hand. You have lent me your hand. I have let you have my hand.

I only want to get intense. A positive meeting of a wolf and a crow would satisfy my recent urges. I want rocks. Oh I want rocks. To be tolerant and sympathetic requires a wolf and a crow and a wolf and a crow. Only a wolf mate can open a crow's eyes to 3 A.M. harmonica and its attendant spirituality. In turn, a wolf's practicality can be a guide, leading wolves to fruition. He turns my dime. He forces my mouth open with his beak and lines my throat with rocks until the water rises. The waters must rise! They rise! Get to me! It is how he gets to my heart. He gets my heart to rise. Raise my dreamy, utopian ideas. Holding each other in a zero gravity chamber, we rock tight. Bring a wolf to fruition.

The best king has a contest with his subjects at all times. This is why there are no great kings. The subjects learn how to self aggrandize and deceive and act like kings themselves. And we are in on the joke. I just wiped a whole plum out of my eye. Kings today have given up and enjoy just hanging out with subjects and having dinner with them instead of involving themselves in the real or imagined conflicts. So no matter what, the subjects are always right because the king has invented these subjects. Therefore, nothing is radical. Everything is in the king's fat head. Even the plum from earlier.

Many times the deer leaves the house in order to interface with society to feel a connection to the world at large. Were you aware of a scientific study which stated that vaginal absorption of semen acts as an anti-depressant in women? The vaginal walls absorb the semen. Another study says that the absorption of the semen through the vaginal walls could increase libido in women. The deer travels from one part of the forest to the next chomping loudly and then quietly. This kind of movement can heal, take the deer out of her body in a lucid dream, or leave her exposed to heroic acts of misogyny.

Sometimes a deer and a wolf combine to form a new being—a being I can't pretend to have the authority or the tools to name. *Deolf?* See? That was terrible. Remember when that car was chasing you and trying to run you over? As you tired you turned around almost ready to give up, and you saw that *you were driving the car*. Talk about a mindfuck. Before falling asleep, put a mirror on the ground so that when you're on the ceiling you can see yourself during lucid dreaming. There is no need to be afraid. No need at all. A grandiose idea sounds like the bump of a lover falling out of bed in the middle of the night.

And well, that's adulthood. You may know it or you may use terms like "work a job while wearing lipstick" or "talking while using italics" to describe it. October is a White Castle Crave Case in the trash. Be a person on the phone, a person's breath warming the electric cradle electrically. Hear a person yelling into the receiver. Yelling has kept me off of phones. When a deer starts something new, she tends to get excited and dive in antlers-first. Many times my approach has backfired, but being the perennial optimist I keep doing it. *Perennial*: a word I have to look up every god-damned time. Constant, recurrent, perpetual, persistent, obtuse. Never use italics in conversation. Revise what is not working.

Something new and exciting is on the horizon. But a horizon requires perspective. Before a deer leaps in, she gets her bearings, her balance. Walk on with an increasing speed toward a desired target. Deer need to learn as much as deer possibly can, create a smart and logical strategy, splice commas, break shit. Invite my corpse on an interview or date. My chaperone will wheel in the coffin ten minutes late. Only then shall you proceed!

Two deer made out. One deer touched his hand tenderly to the other deer's ear such that she felt something unexpected in her chest, something sweet. He delicately touched the edge of her ear—not like he was trying to take something away from her, but like he truly wanted to know something that the sense of hearing cannot convey. This moment played over and over in her mind after the two parted ways. She almost missed her flight. My ear is a small thing that hears the world. And my brain is a thing that processes violence.

Two deer play with their washboard abs. Neither can cook or clean, but they'll drink all the beer and never be cruel to one another. I think that you should date this city dweller. He has a moustache and lots of friends. I can't see him. He isn't here. But that's how he tells you he really loves you. Together, you have the energy to throw your anchor over the edge of the small boat or the tub. The anchor has the decency to not be a metaphor in this instance—it really will keep your boat in one place. You bought a boat. I don't know…it's spiritual. Either get married or leave each other alone.

With a Force More Brutal

WITH A FORCE MORE BRUTAL

I eat alone.
Picnic alone.
Fuck through it all
using my own hands.
Adjustments can lead to personal maturity and evolution.
Lots of food falls out of our hands
and I wonder
whether I have a disease or if I'm dying.
Or why that piece of food—why now?
Time passes.
The food is eaten or is eventually thrown away
or swept into the dust pan.
I close the trash bag
by pulling a red string
strangling its neck
with a force more brutal than I realized I had the capacity for.
But it happens so fast
Would I have the
same brutality were I being
sexually assaulted,

if you tried fucking me

against the wall against my will.

It's funny because I find you attractive, though totally dorky,

and what a strange turn of events – a date rape and murder.

I keep thinking about

cutting holes into walls,

so we can look

at what's real

what's just a monkey

scratching its asshole.

WHAT YEAR ARE YOU INTERESTED IN?

I mean you're not from the
dustbowl
unless you are. Are you?
It's so hard to care
about anything unless one is *in the shit.*
I'm in the shit.

It's impossible for me to write a poem
unless I can wrap my entire chest—
both tits —   in my sadness

It's impossible for me to get out of bed
without a deep pressure.
I feel shame in not doing.

Now, I'll tell you a story about survival.
Once we had a huge fight.

I left Bennigan's while he was in the bathroom
because fuck him, right?

Right?

And I was almost to the corner
(I knew he didn't have even five dollars to pay his tab—
much less the $1.25 to get on the subway home.)
and out of nowhere
I heard three steps
and he pushed me to the ground
like we were in a football game.
And I looked at him
I knew I had to leave him.
He was a dog who pushed a woman to the ground.
He would tell you that it was not the act,
but he was trapped, it was "situational."

He'd say he *heh heh* was the Bernie Goetz
of spousal abuse.

CLICK

A freighter in the distance travels west. The water looks artificial, cobalt. In the foreground the water is white as ice. Seven people stand thigh deep in the water. Six people either look left or right. Two girls look in the direction of the camera unaware of the moment's capture. The one with omega breasts opens her mouth like she's shot.

WE MADE LOVE IN A ROOM WITH THREE GUNS

You don't need a gun to do what we did. The man kept a shotgun at the door and two rifles hidden where no one could see them. The bullets were kept in cases. In fact, everything except the shotgun was secured in a trunk and taken out only during hunting season. Discovering this after a night of lovemaking, the woman stood up and squealed. *I can't believe you didn't tell me!* He laughed.

BUTTER LAMB SPANK BANK

Achilles chased Hector for three laps
And then after he dragged Hector's body
for a number of days from his chariot
He mistreated it and that made him feel better
because Hector had killed his best friend
That's beautiful because it's crystalline
It was not misplaced: he collected and placed clarity everywhere:
around and around the gates of Troy
for days and days and days

Words weren't needed there

Bishop wrote of such a refraction:
everything was rainbow, rainbow, rainbow!
And I let the fish go. (at the moment in which
she chose not to kill in her poem)

A corpse is a fact, but it's not ok

A lamb is a symbol of purest peace
and for generations people have been
killing them and eating them on Easter
and feeling the tender flesh dissolve in their mouths
using words like *melt* and *cum*
Knowing that the lamb had never known another
in a carnal way
And innocence makes us feel good and makes the meat taste better
Maybe because we've each dragged a body to the game

We have felt the flesh and fingered the night
And we need to lift and fill up
our empty degraded chalices with exponential decay
And as if that's not enough
making butter sculptures of lambs too
trim forth something more to spread onto bread

Yet we've cleaved the slaughter from enjoyment

A symbol is a strike with words or images
A beam shot forth from the object into eye
for processing in the brain
and always there's a pillow of air to reduce friction

It's violent to see the red octagon of the stop sign
To feel I've gone too far and must stop
I fear for the butter lamb in danger
of five knives held by family members
and the lazy guy who uses a spoon
and the child's pointer finger
with which he touches everything

Maybe depression is seeing a big stop sign in your mind
breaking hard on violence and anger
Words and action are *something-mumble-something*
And symbols are scary because
a weapon tells you where to go on a map
and "symbols are born and die"

But it's simple brain chemistry.
There's nothing in the ink blot drawing
There was never any meaning there

But also cradle, coffin, mallet, fish hook,
hand, octagon, curdled lamb, corpse curled up in shield,
puck, puke, butter, blot, finger pointing,
butter, finger pointing in butter, lotion, poke,
canine teeth, puke, smell of brain in museum jar,
wash your hands, employees must wash hands

BISECTION AS OBLITERATION

I got a massage once and a few minutes before I came, he unknotted this part of my shoulder that held tension carried on from the end of a relationship.

I sobbed quietly from this unexpected release.

When he divided the pain from my shoulder, he divided it again and again and I thought about how an ex came to drop off books and I cried and was like *Why are you here?*

So he left.

The masseuse divided my pain from itself—tension held in my neck and shoulders—so many times it became so small that I couldn't feel it any more.

One half inch into a quarter inch.

A quarter into an eighth of an inch, and an eighth into I can't feel you anymore.

Invisible, renewed, cleansed like he never happened.

He divided the pain of the book dump from the tears.

He was eating a sandwich as he unknotted my back. He was chewed and chewed.

The tears were also divided into the pain and saline and into laughing at *what a fucking troll* into drinking wine into texting.

When I moved I had to look at, hold, and therefore reckon with each book—*The Complete Tales of Edgar Allen Poe*, *The Complete Novels of Jane Austen*, and tons of sci-fi classics I have since cherished like Arthur C. Clarke's *Childhood's End*.

I tore the Poe in half and put it in my filing cabinet at work.

A year later I threw half of it away because the paper was disintegrating.

Halving is erasing.

Bisection toward obliteration.

He had me on my side and he worked my hip into my labia so that it would rock my clit.

He was professional.

He was also a mouth-breather, but hearing this breath halved silence.

If I make new mistakes I might forget the old ones.

SHOCK SCENE

There is a dead fish in my bedroom
curled up in a bowl. I know a few things
about death and dying.
The water stinks
of furious, hormonal piss.
There is space for me now.
There's space around me now. I feel in life
like film audiences when something
just too shocking happens. Like look at my bruises
as I undress. Like when I watched
The Crying Game with my dad and
oh my god she has a dick. Or like when my dad
and I years later watched Monster's Ball
together and *oh my god she fucks so loud and sad.*
A whole world is born open. My shock scene
has bled over my eternal present.
I grab some gloves and mark it with bleach
and organic cleansers and incense from
the southwest. There is a dead fish in my bedroom
curled up in a bowl. I want to
be loved but I don't know how.

CLICK

A happier sea than before, but the same freighter sails in the distance. Only one woman faces the sea with her eyes raised high to the sky. Sea foam cuts the image in half. It's unclear whether she's trying to touch the sky or the sea foam breaking the waves ahead of her or a perfect horoscope.

A LOVE NO THEORY MAY POSSESS

I can't read about my own desire
spreading its wings across whole cities' blocks
Unfortunately, this cheese that you will have to slice
is just for me, Mr. Deli Guy
The bread I have to buy:
the same
A man driving a truck and I
stared and stared at each other
until I pressed my body
against a heavy door
of a store
just to feel something
just to avoid
feeling something
for a stranger with nice eyes, nice eyes
Deli Guy, see, look what you did there
It's the summer of new sandals
and old bagged romaine
pinking up my fridge
This is a love you've never read about

it squeezes away
a love in no books
that no theory may possess
This is me staring at a cauliflower
a vegetable prominent in the soups of my past
A soft tree, a soft rock plopping in my thoughts
I walk past the family-packs of meat
wrapped in plastic and ready, seated on styrofoam trays
There exists a domesticity beyond one sandwich
for one woman
and the absence of what

HERMENEUTICS

Employees gather in the auditorium. They pull notebooks and pens from briefcases and leather portfolios. Those satisfied with their year-end bonuses partake of the coffee service, which lines the rear wall. Eventually an elephant walked on stage behind a podium and took a giant dump. Some people help themselves to the pastries, but most just keep watching. One intern hotly fingers the corporate logo embroidered onto her leather folio. The elephant stands and crashes over and dies. Some people stand up. Some run from the room. Some just have that *condom broke* look about their faces. Everyone looks around for someone to take control of the situation. Some think the elephant just needs a good doctor. Others are certain of its death. My father stands up and addresses the crowd: *The leaves campaign with vigor each year.*

FROWNING BEAST

A man convinced a woman of his need to be taken care of, for he thought his genius was too significant for certain life details. A year went by and he convinced another woman of his need to be taken care of, for he thought years were women. Each woman was smart and capable. He was neither. Each woman used her resources to help him to further his ambitions putting her own second. Each woman woke up one day with wallet thinner and pussy emptier. Each woman showed him the door, a door that he saw as leading him to the fact of another woman. One day the man walked out of a door and instead of seeing a woman through it, he saw a windy nothing.

LET HIM

I love to see a man's big hand cupping a small book
Its pages fan open and his ring taps
then presses against the hardback cover
I am dimly grieving for an absent silence
He clutches it, precious, reminding me that he is married with his giant metal ring
I love the innocence of a complicated object
held by something so dull and weathered
His fingers are small matte pigs
rough from outside play
or from something nobler
like holding a genius's body
I let him read the new small book
I let him quietly sound the words out with his narrow white lips
He knows these words and he is proud
Let the man read the new book
Do thoughts fill that perfect ken head or is it just a fly caught in a flagon?
Oink goes the piggy in the dark
Oink is a porky mind's surreal *EUREKA!* moment
Cunnilingus ends every great work of art
but sometimes the audience's tongue is flat and dry

A FEELING CAME OVER ME

Sometimes when I walked down First Avenue, a feeling of overwhelming loneliness came over me. In these cases, I walked into a bodega and purchased a small snack. I transacted this business so that the snack belonged to me. It was social. Between Tenth Street and Third Street I would see a man in a wheelchair or a crushed cockroach. The snack kept my body alive a little longer. That was life.

I AM NOT THE SEA

I was sitting outside with friends enjoying the day. The sky was clear and blue. He emerged from the nearest building, walked toward the park, and did not look toward me. He was holding a baseball bat. *Years ago we'd go to the beach. He'd bring a whiffle bat and tape it up multicolor. He'd pick up rocks and hit them into the ocean. I remember the clear Atlantic – its mutual violence and docility. I remember how the rocks dissolved into the sea. The sea took each rock without question. Accepting, almost pleading. If you looked left or right there were always more rocks spat back by its waves. I would stare at him and love him and wonder when his wounds would heal if they would heal at all.* I haven't seen his face in seven years. But here I sat with my friends in the sun. He took the bat and hit something into the air. It landed right on the table I was sitting at, barely missing me. A large crash. I was enraged, for it had been aimed right at me. But I am not the sea. I picked it up and he ran straight at me with a pinched up and pink face. He wanted his rock back. And he was embarrassed that he hadn't killed me. I raised the rock in the air. It was far heavier than I remembered the rocks from the beach. I raised it in the air. It was not a rock, but an hourglass.

FEAR OF MISSING OUT

For months I was anxious about missing out on what the others were doing. I just knew they were having the best time together without me. Then one day I walked by a beach party I'd only just seen in a photo posted on a popular social media website—now here in the flesh—and my suspicions were confirmed. My best friend was dancing with my best bro. Everyone was paired off and laughing in ways so exuberant, their muscles would surely ache for days on days. I had never seen anything like this in my entire life. I said *You guys must be joking. Why didn't you invite me?* The partygoers had no answers, but even in their embarrassment they were still having more fun than I had ever had in my entire life. This party offered such divine gifts, it is impossible to fully describe, but I'll try. My best friend stirred a cocktail containing hand-chipped ice and rum and fresh – *what fruit is that? It smells like ambrosia!* See, once you say no to what they are doing once, they will never invite you to another thing. They snorted gold and hugged puppies without displacing their perfectly coiffed hair. Zero-calorie desserts that taste like thousand-calorie desserts were devoured one after another after another. Spill something on yourself? Who cares! Just get into one of the Jacuzzis and drink lots of expensive champagne. They laughed about their rich & shared past, enjoyed the present moment, and also made plans for their certain & intersecting futures. After that it was just one long, engorged orgasm. One twelve hour long, giant clitoral, vaginal, penile, anus-pulsating, tooth-sucking, foot-stomping orgasm. The kind one can only humanly describe as the experience of doing meth *and* heroin *and* ecstasy while getting fucked doggie style under a beach umbrella with five thousand dollars in your bank account, but not on the sand because that would be uncomfortable. Rather, a twelve hour orgasm of your choice on the beach at night on a clean mattress under the stars but still with the full privacy of knowing that everyone else at the party is also having twelve hour orgasms, and the others are in no way jealous of your twelve hour orgasm because theirs are just so complete. Afterwards, it's brunch for as far as the eye can see.

ARE YOU THE RIGHT GIRL?

two cactus branches pointed at different suns
who's right who's wrong?
myself evaporating
minute into other minutes --
the minutes of later minutes later
pooling into an hour, a puddle.
two things to do on this day:
one is to send a text message intended to have a desired effect,
one is to sit on the self to look inward while using my hands to write.
life is not just reading, drinking green juice, and wearing sweaters anymore.
let it bring you to a party
where someone laughs afterwards,
there is a desired effect a volume claimed by experience and wine
of swishing the self into a clown
and clown into living disaster sculpture with great skin
and wait-for-it, heaving
with lips abloom with oxygenated blood
arms akimbo
standing in the sewer
come here, you over there, it's so lonely in the sewer

when the moon is no longer the moon
we call it the moony moony moon
there's honey on this moon
if you'd just fucking come down here
and hang out in the sewer
it's not just what one thinks, it's the truth
and a collab of experience, time, and fucking a reading list
what does focusing on one item of punctuation do
when the car is traveling seventy-five miles per hour
on a highway without a road beneath tires: only air beneath tires?
a duality of one prickly cactus reaching itself in two different directions
perhaps just the morning of the sun and the evening of the sun
or perhaps be cool girl
who is just mad chill and says "whatever" a lot
and has middling standards
oh women, help me, women
i can see the flexible legs of the ingénue spread open
her cunt tattooed with the words *See me now right now*
but someday
she'll be laying there
and she'll come to know that
all he's done is slap the paint on the brush
while she did all the painting

GOOD BEHAVIOR

I stand in the back row doing nothing with my hands. I won't pull my hair out one strand at a time or mellow out about anything. Let's put a full scale cardboard cut out of an old ugly white male poet in the corner and replace his hand with a wet washcloth for handshaking. Whoever decides that saints are "perfect" & perfection is a goal is wrong. I want to see clearly. I want to see everything clearly. They replaced the wall with a hole.

PROBLEM SOLVING

you look like a dog
but this is a problem worth solving
problem-solving is an adult skill
your "snout" and your tiny eyes are a dog's
you're a dog without ears   who doesn't have ears?
everyone has ears   small-eyed dogs take a really
long time finding out
what space to walk in
on all fours
to walk on all fours   oh how i want to
follow the dog for some time
be jealous of its aching trot
be jealous of its   trot
i imagine myself walking on east 10th street toward the east river   on all fours
your streamlined walk
and how love is
a religion and running is a religion
the east river is the perfect place to dump a body
the cantors pour the wine into the glass
the eunuchs heave their phantom parts

it's safe to say that i have the most irritating phone
in the world   and that i was full of grace last night
diagnosed with twins at 59th street station
obsessive rants on   sky cleavage   butt cleavage   breast cleavage
the other night he couldn't see the hands in front of his face
and i have twins somewhere in my heart below my face
and who cares
you have a baby
and diagnose him
with taking care of you
sometimes i think of when i'm old
and sober when i'm making out
and making out is languid in the birth of sleep
your friend is a housewife
and perhaps even
is a pill problem
i make the same mistakes all the time
some of which
are fixed by technological advances
computers
your dog face is still a problem
but there are many types of dogs
some are quite fluffy and don't have dicks
all men are dogs i suppose

but you really look like one
i don't mean to be cute or sweet
adults still get into rifts
and fights
and need to return to center
their centers are achieved
by recharging a phone
i found a charger that did not belong today
but i couldn't find the russell edson book
that i took out of the library
but while looking for it
i found more potato chip crumbs
in my rug
than you'd think possible

IF HE SAYS HE IS GOING TO BURN DOWN YOUR HOUSE

If he says he is going to burn down your house, you can relax because he's not going to burn down your house. He's just waiting for you to compliment his outfit or is waiting for the "thank you" for helping you get your own house or to fuck you. I hate it when I'm in a building and I know where all the exits are, but the building was built in such a way that I must walk down three splaying corridors of splayed luminosity. I hate to be in pain. I hate pain more than I hate no feelings at all. Once my friend told me that I don't have as wide a palate as her, that I could never enjoy food as much as her because of this. She basically told me I was dead, that I couldn't feel. I remember nodding at her thinking *Bitch has a point!* There is so much out there that has the potential to hurt, but let's admit it, I will never feel as much pain as *certain* other people. I'm going to walk to the café and read a book. It's either that or I flip through each moment. Play it through filmic, on repeat. On repeat for weeks while I can't sleep. Until he's just an entity who said he was going to burn my house down, burn down my house but chose not to.

I ♥ LIFE

We passed a man by the side of the highway with two I ♥ Jesus signs that were bigger than cars and we laughed because his deep need to show those signs to the people on the highway was so passionate and desperate and extreme there was no bodily function besides laughing. He was testifying, sure, but it felt really emotional to us in that moment. Who holds a sign for personal survival? I certainly don't. I love poetry and I love love, but I don't stand in the wind with all my luck. My body will not shut down if I'm not performing a specific duty. Or am I holding an "I ♥ Poetry" sign as I walk around composing lines in my head and notebook? Stealing each subway ride to read a few lines? Is that my big, big sign? Can people read it all over my face? Am I standing on the BQE without even realizing it? Am I in the rain holding on to language? Is my makeup running as pee and blood drip down my leg like a damn animal? Am I pneumonic to you? Is there a virus cracking open, a wet yolk in my eye for all to see? Is there an egg growing out of my flesh? There's a Youtube video of a woman who has raised a duck since it's hatched. It imprinted upon her and now she puts it in cute sweaters with little ♥s on it and it sits on the dashboard when they go out in the car and it watches TV with her when it's night time. When a reporter asked her *Why?* she had a duck living with her, she answered *Why not?* as her whole face lit up like the morning. She was holding an I ♥ sign too. She lives a truth. If she wants to mother a duck, she should. And she does. I don't live as honestly as the I ♥ Jesus sign holder or the Dashboard Duck lady. I want to. But I'm so lazy. And aren't you? The I ♥ life is not to be confused with insanity. It's sanity itself. It's the only. It's love. That heart is not weak.

RAIN

I've found myself staring at the dried grass
As end of summer flops heavy
Like a hydrangea hanging, poised to party
Everything I see is a symbol
for elbowing my way into being noticed on Earth
Every tree I regard is an object of yearning
and so am I
A green light tells me to go
& to cease my idling
but then I think of the new growth leaves
that hue is thieving from
And how that came to be…
And how the blood cells breaking through
the surface of skin
is the symbol of stopping
represents going no further
And how that seems so reasonable
but I am not
In Boston, walking through a graveyard was ordinary

And it's shocking to me when people
have not had this very same experience
You walk around
and read some gravestones
and sometimes you find beautiful names and poems in epitaphs
Olmstead, etc. built these spaces for the visiting
of the dead to be a Pleasant Thing
No one should be alone too long not even the dead
When I first started walking through graveyards as a girl
I was confused to not be holding my breath
since that's what the other kids taught me
It was important to keep the ghosts out when passing by
And god help us when we drove past a railroad track *and* a cemetery
We'd lift our legs, lungs full, puckered lips
These superstitions dragged me unwilling
My laughing parents untwisted me later
I'm sentimental for that good, innocent girl
overcome by superstition
believing anything anyone in power told me
And the bullshit I came up with to explain other things
sounded just as delusional as the truth of the moon growing and shrinking the waves
When I walk through the grass of a graveyard
the grass is different under my feet
It's not only dry

but is a reliquary—that is—
the land itself contains the people
The grass and ivy growth over dirt, over coffins
This is not just grass, it's a symbol for the lives of people
And by walking near these
And hearing the crushing break
that won't grow back
that can't be watered back into life
as the rules of gardening don't apply
& feeling something different
in the quality of this grass that is new *and* dying
I think of dead eye contact with a chewing cow
eye contact I can't forget
the cow eats the hay when there is no fresh grass
& she chews it to crushing noises
and I know that at my worst
I've made that same dead eye contact with my television screen
stuffing fistful after fistful of popcorn into my mouth
And that is not hunger but a way to soothe
the pain of having a human form
And these hands and this mind is what fills it up, what empties
The toppled graves are artifacts
You die, you're buried, a stone commemorates your life and then?
Time passes, the stone falls over, stays there

Keats already wrote this shit before he postured elegantly into his own casket,
before his tissue desiccated into jerky, his waters evaporated into the
    surrounding soil
for us to walk upon, regard and moo at,
for the grass to make the sound of the chewing mouth of the cow
the popcorn falls onto the ground silent, soft between the blades
A Ferris wheel pits my stomach,
I'm in a vertical revolving wheel, my organs unanchored, it feels sexy.
The people are coming all over us, they never left
So you should be afraid not of the cemetery's water bubbler,
but of all the rain

WRITTEN ON HIS DICK

He is the one who drew the 'do not disturb' sign on the door. The cock as the pen and the precum is the ink, obviously. He walked out the door after hearing so much truth and seeing so much mirror. *$ Do not disturb $* I just spent thirty minutes on an internet forum that explained the science behind black light semen detection. Can I send you the link? But he can only write one thing with his regular-sized cock. I wish this were not so. I wish he had more words. I wish he would write many words on all the branches of all the trees like scrolls adorning the Pillars of Hercules. There is one word he can write and when he can't write it, he cries. He wants to write another word but can't. He wants to cry in a different languages, but doesn't.

ENTER SKELETON

He entered my house in pure ivory brilliance clicking his bones awkwardly on the hardwood floor, nodding his head like the most poorly handled stage puppet. One thing that struck me immediately, once I overcame the shine of the thing, was how poised his arms were, macho and casual at his sides. The occasional hand gesture toward where his phone might be in a pocket if he had a phone, as if he had skin and wore clothing. He looked at his wrist and indeed a watch hung loosely—nearly falling off—were it not for the width of the hand bones. The watch's face looked at the floor, so he lifted the watch over his wobbling head to get the time. "It's FIVE-THIRTY," I yelled just so he would stop. I asked him to have a seat, which he did, and he remarked that my couch was uncomfortable to sit on. Though he was right, I wondered what he might have to compare it to. The purpose of the buttocks is to protect against such discomforts, and he was plainly not in possession of a butt. "Are you alive?," I asked sighing. "No," he answered cheerfully. "Are you of polished ivory?" I asked even though he was clearly a human skeleton. He looked up at me. He held his head still and said, "Why-do-people-ask-things-that-they-know-are-not-so?" slowly, quietly. Tears came to my eyes. "This is no time for a breakdown. I can not give that to you today." So, the silence continued for years until I asked for the opposite of what I had asked first.

THE ONLY DEAD GUY HERE IS YOU!

Pointing in agreement I then curled my hand beneath my chest. Playing is serious. It hardens the heart with the gravity of Jupiter. The curled hand is now fisted, cutting across the air, fisted. Don't point, I say to myself—raise my eyebrows to make a fuss. Some lady said that pointing is not polite. Turns out her assault shared a plot with an episode of *Three's Company*: naked bodies rushing forth in different directions, an elaborate dinner that never gets eaten, towns like fig leaves, and a shrub just a smidgen smaller than a human form. Turns out you pointed in agreement to your own heart, with your own self. In gravity two and a half times her previous atmosphere, she can't run so fast anymore…or hide. My psychologist friend said this happens as a result of uhh intersubjectivity, the dynamic between two or more people plus some bad or questionable decisions and a few more things like setting or… uhhh….Something about being a woman prods me away from describing this with genuine confidence. Fuck psychology. It's only a matter of time before we two meet the way adults do! Sometimes I am two male oryx at a big table mixing up the sacred fruit of my gelding, why just look: weave fabric with sexy needle antlers. I'm un-fisted, flat palm downward, showing off my new manicure, clapping for the first time in my life! I don't mean to sound flirty, but uhhh um, well I prefer to Google "How long is Led Zeppelin's song Kashmir?" over listening to an eight minute and twenty-eight second orgasm that I am not a part of…Last night my mother walked into my childhood bedroom, touched the left side of my forehead to see if I was home, to see if I was really there. She touched to know. I always respond to being touched—I shake my head, say *What the…?*

LITTLE CUNT

I don't want to be right
I just want to roll down a hill
like a log
in the arboretum
into a laughing frenzy
One time
he spat in my face
after I was
already crying
and as I lay
pressed against
the wall I wanted to roll right through
and into the Jamaica Pond and die
I thought dying would be my escape from him
I thought about dying a lot
Instead I am right here
I'm right here, New York
alive
where *la de fuckin da*
where it is nothing to be

precious over
a step beyond survival to
laugh breathe fuck
join-the-fucking-club culture
I read my dustbowl poem twice
at poetry readings
this month
and the second time I thought he'd
materialize through the walls
& throw a dart
into my eye killing me
and the obit would read:

> *That fucking cunt*
> *That little tight cunt*
> *didn't know who she was*
> *but I showed her*
> *I showed her*

It is hard to be a person
who's made mistakes
because I forget most of the time
that I was indeed a scared little cunt
because now I write poems
and hang out with my friends

who love my loud laugh
and the scared little cunt
crying with spit in my face
who couldn't get fucked properly
Oh so help you god if you ever mention me in a poem
isn't what they see me as
They would scarcely believe
how much he made me cry
the volume of my tears
and how scared I was
how dumb he made me feel
or how much I cooked for him
and how I loved him with my whole self
No matter how much anaphora I use
if they took one look at me
they wouldn't recognize me
But today
I saw a photograph of myself
sleeping in a crib
when I was a baby
and I was happy to see
she is still me
innocent me
peacefully

A CERTAIN DIGNITY

There is nothing to say. I live in a present previously unseen. To get any attention, I used to throttle myself in front of people. But now I don't want the attention and have no way of murdering myself into the proper shape. This is my dignity. I observe how people breathe silently out of their functioning nostrils (the universal). I describe the cute guy who folds into himself while reading a novel in the café (the particular).

THE WAY YOU GRAB A BIRD

Those who ought to alight on the exposé on death
are hungry like a parking meter for an intolerable currency, fist, and breath.
I have evidence that my breath is wet. I have no choice.
I've been talking to the dead.
I have a human body for my mailing address.
As mother and master to my body,
I listen to a music bird that pings my soul, it pokes
aside my passions, sure as this bird, a brother of a living Ggodd,
a trust, companion breath is me. It resonates further with the addition
of more banking language inserted herein.
Perk your ears up when reminded of money and also the workplace,
familiar things help one to listen, and close my ears without context,
need sampling. Now it's time, aging looks really hard, feels hard,
but the older I become, the older Ashbery is,
the softer my body feels even on the insides.
I'm revolted by the word 'juice' today, its secretions, and I am thinking
about intimacy after brunch & for all the brunch consumed in the U.S.,
thinking about Aretha, her finger wagging, warning us with her fortitude & vision,
thinking about the chafing of iron against iron without heat,
how that's New York, throwing myself against the world,

the sheer balls on something that does not end,
that provides no answers, novels are like that, really good novels.
It's always someone's birthday when I wear a mask.
A hole opened in the sidewalk due to some shit that happened deep within
the earth's crust, the crust divides my sidewalk chapel,
please find a really good German phrase for that,
we walkers we swing our eyes down,
inviolable, it opens and pink emerges, it's a pussy,
it is the wet of an eye, it hunts, the opposite of an eraser, it can't yet cease,
it's just begun because it mothers me, all justice is gone
when the mother is speaking because she is a mother,
she's pussy on the ground, floors go indoors,
vaginas have walls not floors,
and the heat of nature does not submit to the buildings of man,
skyscrapers are man's attempts to control the mother, futile,
this has been said before but bears repeating, with tongue,
that you can not control a mother. Grab me, scrape,
the way you'd grab a bird, gentle but with a muscular accuracy
and gentler hands, saying that all a bird does is fly is as inaccurate.
If I surrender completely to your touch,
then I am charged to fly away and thus.

BEAUTY BERRIES

My mom showed me some Beauty Berries:
berries you only see once the greenery has been shed.
The berries are revealed after the bush had sloughed its leaves through a death cycle.
Sometimes a gift or a beautiful idea
is hidden until some action occurs
or in the case of leaves: death, weather
changes, and time.
Carter's mom asked me if I was still single because I was so powerful
and that stabbed me in the gut
while also flattering me.
I've often thought that getting stabbed by a knife would feel warm like this.
Like the moment I reached down to my crotch
and felt some blood
fuck I knew this was going to happen today
but the stabbing was somewhere else
and the warmth was just as warm.
My leaves fall away.
My workouts burn hundreds of calories
and my burial will cost between eight and twelve thousand dollars,
which I have not even begun to start to save for.

THE SICK CITY

If something bad happens, where do you turn?
By turning, a lot can happen, but it can take a long time.
We turn in slow motion.
These hollow years we crane our necks, leaning.
Don't miss one tiny, itsy, little, important bit!
When you turn toward someone, a secret undoes.
Its petals puke forth from my gentle wound mouth.
I think of the whole city I left
its germs of regret and failure cams.
I think this in a city I move through with more adult problems, more failure.
The loneliness felt at age sixteen, these words fell onto my journal: *Dear diary,*
  I don't get it.
Dear diary, I am so alone.
Spoken in the mock meek voice of a boneless, amorphous spinster.
Take the 38 or the 51, the Needham Heights line from Roslindale Village
  to Back Bay,
or the Orange Line to Forest Hills. The head turned left to see the
  approaching vehicle.
But I left the hometown. The beach chairs are folded up in the cellar.
It's been ages since I groped in the dark for my R's.

Now I throw on my trill shades, hold to temporary and lasting friendships, but
sleep alone.
My arrowcursor touches many faces, but the darkness candle lit in Boston
stalks my feet.
Dear Diary, I still don't get it.
I've felt love in heat with learned hotheads, blaming denim shirts in the night.
A manic teen's fragrant sticker portfolio. I have a lost cashmere statue's dedication.
We are looking at apples. I proffer some fucked up shit, question every move.

How many dollar beers does it take? How can I be ethical and also love?
You're no detective.
On TV everyone is on one trajectory towards a steamy sleepless night.
I've not been shredded lately.
I want to paint you with your fingers until the darkness lit in Boston gives me
brand new feet.
A phone leak: phone calls like they're normal. I know who I love, but it's
never convenient.
I know the story that I tell. It's no lamer than yours.
Let me go through your skin organ: below the chains and above the organs.
Below the clothes and over the skin.
Let me go over your life's work: I'm holding your brain and crying.
Admiration and creepiness and admiration and creepiness and walking backwards
I exit
through the same door through which I arrived: a nod, a step, a nod toward a step.

The devil can pass right through us if you use more than one door.

My Nana was full of this kind of shit. But I will not go back in my Mama's vagina.

No this isn't *my kind* of autopsy: I'm alive burning.

It's crazy to think this way by continuing to associate with the dying or dead.

It doesn't matter: I'm prodigal.

I'm in the sick city making love. With whom?

I'm in the sick city making love to an idea.

I'm in my grazing years but holding no gold or inheritance.

And I won't. There's no beautiful material to lose.

I wouldn't say any of this if my body won Gold in the touching Olympics.

I'd like to put you in a sling and swing your broken hand back and forth shaking it.

That hurt? How about that? Does that hurt? How about right here?

I'd like to put you in a hammock, rock you and love, waving *Bye Felicia!*

I broke your hand. That was me. Happy, happy birthday.

Happy birthday, I broke your hand. I'm still turning toward you,

communicating more, more like the bloody sun as time passes, with each
passing minute.

It's hard to understand but the touch of your hand can start me crying.

Grateful, loving, and special thank you to my family: Carol Lawless, James Lawless, Carol Miranda Lawless, and especially Molly Lawless. I love you.

Thank you to my friends Chris Cheney, Jackie Clark, Ora Colb, B.C. Edwards, Dan Hoy, Christine Kanownik, Ben Mirov, Paige Taggart, Sampson Starkweather, Maggie Wells, and Angela Veronica Wong.

Special thank you to Hajara Quinn, Zachary Schomburg, Drew Scott Swenhaugen, and Mathias Svalina at Octopus Books for their loving care, stewardship in the birth of this book.

Thanks to the publishers and editors of *Ampersand Review*, *The Atlas Review*, *Birdfeast*, *Bone Bouquet*, *The Common*, *Equalizer (Second Series)*, *Hot Metal Bridge*, *Hyperallergic*, *iO Poetry*, *notnostrums*, *Similar:Peaks*, *Smoking Glue Gun*, *Valley Voices: A Literary Review*, *The Volta*, *Washington Square Review*, where poems and excerpts have appeared. Special thanks to Kelly Schirmann and Black Cake Records for publishing an audio chapbook *from BROADAX*.

FRANZ KAFKA

A BOOK MUST BE THE AXE FOR THE FROZEN SEA WITHIN US. THAT IS MY BELIEF.